# THE

# JIMI HENDRIX

BY
Tom Stockdale

|||•PARRAGON•|||

This edition first published by Parragon Books Ltd in 1995

Produced by
Magpie Books Ltd, London

Copyright © Parragon Book Service Ltd 1995
Unit 13–17, Avonbridge Trading Estate
Atlantic Road
Avonmouth
Bristol BS11 9QD

Illustrations courtesy of: Rex Features.

ISBN 0 75250 684 6

A copy of the British Library Cataloguing in Publication
Data is available from the British Library.

Typeset by Hewer Text Composition Services, Edinburgh
Printed in Singapore by Printlink International Co.

# Birth Of A Wild Man

In 1942, Al Hendrix was in the United States Army. He was not in Seattle with his young wife, Lucille, on 27 November, when she gave birth to a son, and named him John Allen Hendrix. In fact, when Al did return, three years later, the boy had been fostered out to a family, as Lucille could not cope on her own. Al took John back, and on 11 September 1946, in a gesture of starting afresh, renamed him James Marshall Hendrix.

James was a quiet boy, and had an uneventful childhood. His abiding passion from an early age was music, and, because guitars were always around in the homes of friends, the instrument became his favourite. His main influence was the blues of the greats, such as Muddy Waters and B B King, but he was open to the rock 'n' roll of the 1950s, and he taught himself to play through listening to a wealth of different styles. His left-handedness would provide the odd visual effect of playing a right-handed guitar upside-down, and his eclectic influences continued to present a sound that mimicked none of them.

His first gigs were as a member of a covers band while he was in High School, and when he dropped out aged 17 and joined the army, to avoid the draft, his guitar went with him. He made 25 parachute drops as a private in the 101st Airborne, before breaking his ankle and receiving an honourable discharge. He always counted himself lucky at having got out just before the Vietnam War started. While in the army, he formed a band called The King Kasuals with fellow serviceman Billy Cox, and after his discharge he continued playing with Cox and other Rhythm & Blues outfits around the southern United States, until, tired of a static scene in Tennessee, he moved up to New York.

Soon after moving, he won $25 in an amateur music contest, and met 'Faye' Prigeon, a Harlem club regular, with whom he struck up an immediate bond. He moved in with her, and soon her network and his musical prowess came together. The Isley Brothers arrived in town and needed a guitarist – Hendrix was given an audition and the job. The fruits of his time with the Isley Brothers appeared on six recorded songs in 1964/5, though none of them was a hit, during a time when The Beatles and The Rolling Stones were taking turns at the top of the charts. His duties as a sideman did not stretch him, however, and, bored, he soon dropped out, to play with a variety of bands. His Rhythm & Blues talent was noticeable by now, and the names he played behind make impressive reading: B B King, Jackie Wilson and Sam Cooke, Ike and Tina Turner, Little Richard, Wilson Pickett and King Curtis. But again, he quickly tired of each job, and it was obvious that he needed to have more control over what he played. His first such experience came in late 1965 when he joined Curtis Knight and The Squires.

With Curtis Knight, he gained his first songwriting credits, and had more access to studios during the band's attempts to crack the record charts – though the plethora of recordings that have been released from Hendrix's tenure with the band belies its brevity. During one gig at the Cheetah Club, he was noticed by Linda Keith, British fashion model and girlfriend to Keith Richards, who could not believe that someone of his skills was playing such a background role in a band. She was determined to use her contacts to help Hendrix win some financial backing, and with her help he gathered a band

together which he called Jimmy James
and The Blue Flames.

At this time Hendrix was noticeably shy
about his singing, feeling that his voice
would be unacceptable in comparison
with the tones of his blues heroes. Keith
tried to persuade him otherwise, realizing
that his lack of confidence was actually
rooted in his Cherokee and Afro-Amer-
ican heritage. The Blue Flames were a
collection of whites from Greenwich Vil-
lage, and the gigs they booked were local
to the area. Hendrix wanted to develop a
style that gave vent to his personal and
musical background, but it would have to
hit the spot with an audience too.

Linda Keith arranged a showcase with
Andrew Loog Oldham, manager of The

Rolling Stones, for which she 'liberated' a white Fender Stratocaster from Keith Richards. Oldham did not take the bait, nor did other influential contacts. But in July 1966, an introduction to Animals' bassist and hopeful producer Chas Chandler set Hendrix onto the fast lane. The Animals were in America for a farewell tour, after which Chandler wanted to scout for new acts to break. Hearing Hendrix at the Café Wha was all it took for Chandler to offer Hendrix a trip to London, an offer which received a positive, if guarded, 'fair enough'. It was not as if America had 'discovered' Hendrix, or even paid him at more than a subsistence level wage, and British music had recently stormed America, with The Beatles leading the charge.

Although Chandler's musical success had not made him rich, he was able to arrange an advance of cash from his parent company, Yameta, to pay for Hendrix's uprooting. There was more of a problem with a passport, there being no record of Hendrix's birth, until his original name was discovered. On 24 September 1966, Hendrix left New York without a work permit, and with many doubts concerning his acceptance in London. On arrival, he managed to get a seven-day visa, and to allay his fears, Chandler took him immediately to a three-hour jam, with a much impressed blues player, Zoot Money. And this was day one! A week later, on 1 October, through Chandler having bumped into Eric Clapton and Jack Bruce, Hendrix was invited to play with Cream at their Regent Polytechnic gig.

Within the first few bars of Howlin' Wolf's 'Killin' Floor', Clapton's mouth had dropped open, and his subsequent regular visits to Chandler's flat, where Hendrix now lived, was an obvious endorsement of the new talent in town.

Britain was rocking to the sounds of The Beatles' *Revolver* as Chandler set about auditioning a band for Hendrix. Ex-Loving Kind rhythm guitarist Noel Redding was persuaded to switch to bass, and Hendrix liked enough of what he saw to want him in the band. Redding's red frizzy hair was similar in style to Hendrix's, which gave potential to the visual aspect, and his lack of experience with the instrument gave Hendrix the opportunity to develop Redding's playing with his own style. Drummer Mitch Mitchell had both rock and jazz experience, most notably with Georgie Fame and the Blue Flames. His technical expertise would become more and more apparent as the band grew, testing Hendrix's limits in a musical competition, but the ball always came right back into Mitchell's court, as the guitarist's skills coped with and in turn challenged the drummer. And there was no need to recruit another guitarist, as Hendrix's playing was versatile enough to fill all the gaps.

The band was finalized just in time, for Hendrix's jam at Blaise's club caught the attention of French star Johnny Hallyday, who invited him to back him on a tour of France starting ten days later. With minimal rehearsing, a name change from Jimmy to Jimi, and the decision to call the band the Jimi Hendrix Experience, they were off. Their short, blazing sets were acclaimed by the audiences, with a finale at the giant Olympia in Paris. The power of the trio was largely due to the showmanship of its frontman, gained from his years on the road, playing with one hand, behind his back, on his head, even with his teeth.

Returning to England, The Experience played several showcase gigs at clubs which drew the music industry's key players. With the social network of Linda Keith, and word of mouth from those who had witnessed the new phenomenon, Hendrix was being tested at the highest level, and he passed with distinction. Members of The Beatles, The Stones and The Who came backstage, and the respect

Jimi Hendrix

Jimi was guitarist for the Isley brothers for a time

that he was shown helped Hendrix's confidence – a boost which must have put into thankful perspective the initial press interest, which revolved more around descriptions of him as the 'Wild Man of Borneo', and a 'Mau Mau' than as a musician of amazing skill. Britain had not witnessed a black rock musician before, especially one who played with such flamboyant virtuosity, and the choice of two white Britons behind him made a statement before the band had even played a note. The acceptance of his musical peers was therefore an important indicator for anyone serious about checking out the music behind Hendrix's immediate press profile.

In between gigs and rehearsals, the band recorded 'Hey Joe', the song which had

most struck Chandler when he first saw
Hendrix. It was Jimi's first vocal recording,
and Chandler's first production job, and
the result made it obvious that both had
made the right decision in joining up
together. 'Hey Joe' was backed with
Hendrix's first original composition,
'Stone Free', and there was immediate
evidence of the energy and the potential
of The Experience. The distinctive sound
was sold at the Scotch of St James club,
when Track Records co-owner Kit Lam-
bert saw a perfect act for his left-field label.
The deal was struck then and there,
although because the label was not quite
ready, 'Hey Joe' was released on Polydor
in time for the Christmas market on 16
December 1966, with the top of the charts
seeing Tom Jones' 'Green Green Grass of
Home' take over from The Beach Boys'

'Good Vibrations'. Hendrix's under-
ground exposure, and a Track Records-
organized appearance on the television
programme *Ready Steady Go!* three days
before, helped the hard-edged single get a
wider coverage and it entered the charts at
number 38, peaking at number 4. Meanwhile, the 'Wild Man' press image was
turned to advantage as the country's youth
took Hendrix's visual style to its rebellious
hearts, and the single's ascent warranted a
performance on *Top of the Pops*.

Hendrix had been unleashed, and followed his first self-penned song with
'Purple Haze/51st Anniversary', songs
which saw the studio team searching for
technical answers to the musical questions
which Jimi's innovation posed. More gigs
followed, including backing The New

Animals and a prestigious show at the Saville Theatre supporting The Who, another Track Records signing. By the end of January 1967, Hendrix had taken just four months to win over London's musical elite.

# London

When Chas Chandler brought Jimi Hendrix to London, he had talked business with Animals' manager, Mike Jeffery. Jeffery was an astute nightclub owner who had utilized an offshore tax-haven for his wards in the pursuit of an advantageous situation for the sometimes short, if very sweet, lifetime of a rock band. The two agreed to share a management deal with Hendrix, with Jeffery seeing to financial needs and

Chandler providing the personal and technical supervision. The relocation of Hendrix in London had cost the pair a fair amount of money, and had also included Jeffery's buying-out of contracts that Hendrix had entered into in America – not an easy task, as Jimi had no copies of anything, and did not seem to have considered important the length of a contract after the initial project for which it was signed.

With Hendrix signed to Yameta, Jeffery's Bahamas-based tax-shelter, Jeffery and Chandler looked forward to sharing a healthy 40 per cent of Hendrix's financial gain. Jeffery followed up leads to sign him through Yameta to an American record company. (Redding and Mitchell were only ever on a wage, and though it was a 50–25–25 split with Hendrix for fees, there was never any doubt as to who the star was.)

Jeffery had left instructions with his New York lawyers to look into the possibility of a deal with Warner/Reprise, and while the Jimi Hendrix Experience continued touring, and recorded 'The Wind Cries Mary' with one eye on the hourly rate (Chandler had been pawning his guitars to ensure that Hendrix's ideas could be committed to tape), possibility became reality. In a deal which consolidated Jeffery's negotiating reputation, Warner put up a $20,000 promotional budget, a $40,000 advance, and a soundtrack exclusion, whereby Warner would not have any rights to a film score by their new artist. The size of the deal was big enough by normal standards, but this one was not only signed through a third agency (Yameta), but was for an artist whose band had released nothing in America. What's more, Yameta retained ownership of the recordings.

'Purple Haze' was released on 27 March 1967, entering the charts at number 37, and, with the influx of money from Warner, Chandler could afford to take The Experience to a better quality studio to continue recording. At Olympic Studios they met Eddie Kramer, a well-respected engineer, who seemed to understand Hendrix immediately. Although Chandler had the overall production responsibilities, Hendrix was beginning to focus more on the actual sounds he was trying to fix on tape and Kramer was able

Noel Redding and Mitch Mitchell joined
Hendrix to form The Experience

Jimi arrived in London at the height of the
flower-power craze

to translate his vocabulary of thoughts and colours, arranging the recordings to facilitate Hendrix's desire to overdub without losing the original backing section – not an easy thing to do on a four-track machine. With the pressing need to prepare material for a debut album, which would not contain any of the band's single releases, there was suddenly the right team to make it work.

In the meantime, Chandler had got the group a place on the Walker Brothers tour, with Engelbert Humperdinck and Cat Stevens. The first two acts had got to number 1 in the last year, so Hendrix was guaranteed a record-buying audience. At the Astoria gig, Hendrix set his guitar alight with lighter fuel for the first time, causing a sensation amongst the crowd and winning national news coverage. It helped the second single climb to number 3 in the charts. However, the audience reaction on the tour caused more than a little aggravation from the headliners, who were being upstaged not only by the music and the show, but by increasing numbers of female fans, attracted amongst other things, to the psychedelic clothes which Hendrix was now wearing. The experimental ethos of American flower-power had arrived in London, and Hendrix's colour, dress, showmanship and musical originality made him a natural figurehead for a youth which would rally to anyone considered outrageous by the older generation.

During and after the tour, sessions continued for the album. Songs like 'Foxey

Lady' and '3rd Stone from the Sun' had appeared like magic out of previous sessions, often starting with a riff that Chandler would call attention to during a jam, sometimes based on ideas that Hendrix had worked out beforehand. The volume of quality material that he was coming up with took everyone by surprise, and at Olympic Studios numbers from the live sets such as 'Fire' and 'May This Be Love' were polished by the different elements of the team. Redding's solid basslines gave Mitchell a chance to show more of his jazz influence, and Hendrix impressed them all with the sounds that he could squeeze out of the strings. Just after 'The Wind Cries Mary/ Highway Chile' was released in Britain, and 'Hey Joe' in America, *Are You Experienced?* was brought out on 14 May and leapt to number 3 in the album charts. And at the beginning of June, with the help of a good word from Hendrix fan Paul McCartney, The Experience were booked to make their first American appearance at the Monterey festival, on the 18th of that month.

Upon their arrival in America, Jeffery, realizing that a single live date was not going to be enough to break a band which had only put one single, organized a booking agency, a merchandising company and a publicity agent for The Experience. In London, Chandler's contacts were an obvious promotional asset, but America held no such advantages. There was a great deal to be won or lost from the Monterey appearance, and the band was billed to follow the spectacular instrument-destroying demonstration of The Who. In reply, Hendrix led The Experience on a masterclass of live entertainment. He brought all of his showmanship into play for a gale-force 'Like a Rolling Stone', the anthem-in-the-making 'Purple Haze', and a definitive version of The Troggs' 'Wild Thing', ending with a guitar burning and breaking that left the crowd breathless, and which was caught forever by the cameras recording the event.

The performance gained The Experience a run of dates with Jefferson Airplane and Big Brother and The Holding Company at the Fillmore West, together with an unannounced free show in Golden Gate Park in San Francisco. They played and partied their way into the hearts of the city, and it was during this visit that

Hendrix was introduced to the dangerous pleasures of LSD. Although more dates were added, including a Central Park gig that gave Hendrix the chance to show his old friends what he had achieved since leaving the country, Mike Jeffery had set up a tour backing The Monkees. Everybody was shocked by his matching of Jimi's music with that of the 'pre-fab four', but they were obliged to fulfil the contract. Touring was the main way to keep the cash flowing, and there was a lot of money being spent on promoting Hendrix as a major contender.

After some studio sessions which captured, most notably, 'The Burning of the Midnight Lamp' on tape, the tour got under way, with the teenage fans crying for The Monkees almost before Hendrix had fin-

Jimi's first stage appearances met with
sensational acclaim

The Experience on stage

ished his first solo. An escape plan was
hatched, and The Experience were able to
leave the tour part-way through by claiming that they had been threatened with
legal action by the vigilantes of moral
rectitude, the Daughters of the American
Revolution. Although the story was fake,
it was not questioned, and in fact got the
band national press coverage and a healthy
counter-culture reputation amongst the
politically aware youth of the flower-
power movement.

There was, however, one disadvantage in
Hendrix's sudden rise to commercial
viability. This came in the shape of Ed
Chalpin and his PPX Industries. Hendrix
had signed a three-year contract with
Chalpin in 1965, when he was with
Curtis Knight, and Jeffery had not

known of it when he was clearing up
Hendrix's outstanding obligations early
in 1967. Chalpin filed lawsuits claiming
exclusive rights to all Hendrix's music,
including the flood of ideas which
Chandler and Jeffery had helped to
make possible. To complicate matters
even further, Hendrix went to see his
old band in New York in July 1967 and
participated in two recorded jam sessions,
which gave Chalpin indisputable evidence of brand new PPX/Hendrix demos (in addition to tapes from 1965). If
Hendrix had thought he could jam with
old friends covered only by a spoken
agreement to keep his name out of any
vinyl result, he was naively unaware of
the commercial power that his name now
carried. The fact that he was blowing
headliners like Scott MacKenzie and

the Mamas and the Papas off the stage at the Hollywood Bowl should have made that obvious.

# Hot Property

The Experience returned to London at the
end of August 1967, to see 'The Burning
of the Midnight Lamp' charting at number
29 in a country whose state of happy
confusion over the lyrics of Procul Har-
um's number 1 'A Whiter Shade of Pale',
was matched by their enjoyment of the
hip cinema release *Blow Up*. The band was
getting regular press and television attention now, and could charge more for gigs,
which meant that they could afford to

return to the studio to catch up on making permanent records of their progress. Work was begun on material for the follow-up to *Are You Experienced?* and Hendrix spent more time in the studio, dissatisfied with note-perfect songs which no one else could see any problem with. Eddie Kramer's rapport with Hendrix continued to be of immense value to him, although he was starting to take more control behind the mixing desk, but Chas Chandler was more impatient with the constant overdubbing, and aware that his role was becoming more that of facilitator than producer.

Hendrix's reputation was also making the organization of sessions more difficult, not only with the number of musicians who wanted to play on sessions, but also with hangers-on, who, as well as providing a distraction outside the studio, were more likely to continue the party inside it. Songs like 'If Six Was Nine' and 'She's So Fine' needed little work, as they had been demoed for the first album, but the new work was more complicated and there were more instruments being tried out for them, as well as custom-made effects which Hendrix had got from Roger Mayer, an electronics enthusiast who helped satisfy the guitarist's demand for innovation. Hendrix was keen to make the records a different experience from the live sound; 'EXP' and 'One Rainy Day' were songs that would rarely be heard live because of this. The track 'Bold as Love' featured an early phasing technique with which he was so pleased that the finished album *Axis: Bold as Love* would be named

after the song. The only major glitch
before the release of the album was that
Hendrix left the master of side one in a
taxi, after going to a party. With no safety
copy having been made, the team was
forced to remix the whole thing over-
night from the multi-track, compressing
what had been days of work into just a few
hours.

What would prove to be The Experience's last British tour got them through
November and early December, as *Axis:
Bold as Love* entered the album charts at
number 8, while The Beatles' *Sergeant
Pepper's Lonely Hearts Club Band* rode the
top of the charts. More studio work in
December laid the foundations for the
next album; it also exposed the cracks
between Hendrix and Chandler, which

had been widened by Chandler's opposition to Hendrix's drug-taking. Marijuana and speed had regularly been a part of Hendrix's socializing, but his introduction to LSD in America had come as a surprise to Chandler. Although Jimi could not handle much alcohol, his drug intake seemed to grow with the increasing number of parties at which he was a welcome and enthusiastic guest. The disruptive power of LSD came between the two friends, and their working relationship fell apart.

There was more commercial disruption caused in December by the American release of *Get That Feeling: Curtis Knight Sings, Jimi Hendrix Plays*, which Ed Chalpin had licensed to Capitol Records. It was marketed to emphasize sideman

Hendrix over bandleader Knight, and confused the public into buying what they thought was the new Hendrix album, not a collection of old songs and the more recent demos. The January release of *Axis: Bold as Love* in the United States suffered from the confusion, despite negative reviews of *Get That Feeling* and a successful injunction against its misleading cover, but it still reached number 75 in the charts, selling albums which the Hendrix camp felt strongly were of a standard well below that with which he wanted fans to associate him. In addition, the injunction would not stop Chalpin from making other releases until Hendrix's three-year contract with him expired in October 1968.

In January 1968 Hendrix got out of control on a Swedish tour, and he was arrested after a hotel fight. He was allowed to play the concerts, but had to report daily to the police station, and was released with a fine only due to the help of Swedish family connections of Chandler. The band left London to its diet of *The Sound of Music* and flew to New York, which had been decided upon as the new base for The Experience, despite Chandler, Redding and Mitchell's preference for the London life. Jeffery considered the British nut to have been cracked, and the American kernel promised a lot more oil. He had set up a lengthy tour, putting into place a mould-breaking promotional plan, in which the system of local agents booking concerts for a band was replaced by fewer agencies taking a larger area, for a smaller percentage, yet a larger net gain. This meant that The Experience took a

The Experience supported The Who
in London

Hendrix off stage

greater percentage of the profit, and could also be assured of a better organized and more comfortable tour.

The Experience roared into San Francisco on a bill with Albert King and John Mayall's Bluesbreakers, and set off around the country with backing which included Eric Burden's Animals, Soft Machine and The Electric Flag, whose drummer, Buddy Miles, was a friend of Jimi's from the Isley Brothers days. The tour gave the band very few days off, and the post-gig parties were almost clichés of rock excess; in Philadelphia a group of girls arrived at the band's hotel to 'pay their respects' with clothes painted onto their naked bodies. There was also a degree of racial trouble, most notably in Texas, where the show was stopped by a stage invasion.

Back in New York after a well-deserved holiday, Hendrix settled in to a Manhattan scene of club jams and after-hours sessions, including one with a stoned Jim Morrison taking the microphone in an exhibition of obscenity which was recorded for posterity.

The Record Plant was chosen as the studio to work in; it had Gary Kellgren as an engineer, whom Hendrix had worked with previously, and one of the first twelve-track machines in the country. Its producer, Tom Wilson, persuaded Eddie Kramer to come over to the States to add his reputation to the new studio's pulling power. He arrived in the middle of April, and they got straight down to work.

The heavy touring schedule had filled the coffers, so there was no need to watch the clock, which was a good job, since Hendrix wanted to make the next album in his own time, and his labour-intensive recording needs were increased by the stream of onlookers he could not bring himself to bar. 'Little Miss Strange' and 'Gypsy Eyes' were brought to a satisfactory state, but the tensions in the studio were more obvious than ever. Hendrix had got his own flat, and had lost the rapport with Chandler that had grown in London. Redding and Mitchell were also doing their own thing, and Jeffery was not helping by bringing round different drug samples for Hendrix to share. Chandler decided to abandon any production work on what had turned into a double album, and would continue to have involvement only on the managerial side of The Experience.

A Fillmore East concert in May with Sly and the Family Stone won acclaim from the critics, but the profits from the show, along with other assets, were frozen by a court order set up by PPX. Jeffery had tried to buy out Chalpin with a $70,000 offer, but Chalpin could see for himself, now that Hendrix was based in America, the sort of earning potential that he might be able to share.

The battle between PPX and Yameta came to court in May 1968, with both sides claiming their right over Hendrix. Warner was standing on the sidelines, until it was pointed out to them that their contract was with Yameta, not with

Purple Haze

Hendrix. If Yameta lost, they lost. The very next day a gaggle of corporate lawyers thrashed out a settlement, giving PPX a percentage of all Hendrix's profits until 1972, and giving Yameta control of any Hendrix material released by PPX. Chalpin was also guaranteed an album of Experience material for release by Capitol. The agreement gave Warner a buy-out of the Yameta/Hendrix contract, and an exclusive deal with the artist, for which they paid $450,000. Although Chandler and Jeffery still held managerial positions in the new order, with healthy percentages attached, Chandler decided to go back to England to find new bands to produce, and would remain bitter about the way Jeffery treated Jimi as an asset rather than the artist Chandler had helped him to become.

# Electric Ladyland

Back at the Record Plant more work was completed on the album, including the first credits to Buddy Miles, who had become a regular at the studio. The daytime sessions were for serious work with Kramer, and the nights were used for jamming, inspiration, or just not turning up. When they were jamming, the tape would simply be left running, a tactic which resulted in piles of unusable tapes, but which allowed any spark to be captured for a more serious look. The experimentation allowed for all sorts of different combinations and techniques to be tried out, and the most successful ones found their way onto *Electric Ladyland*. The array of influences showed Hendrix's appetite for any style of music, and put him in a completely different league from most rock bands, who tended to stick to a winning formula.

Hendrix's musical eclecticism reflected his general political stance. He could show sympathy with extremists like the Black Panther movement, as well as with the peaceful ideals of the flower-power culture, and was an individualist, not allied to a specific school of thought.

The best way for Hendrix to make his feelings known was through the songs he wrote. Although he was aware that his audience-base was primarily white, he made attempts to bring his musical vision of society to the black community in New York, without being used by the polarizing forces of straight, political statement. His biggest difficulty came from lack of crossover between black and white musical outlets. Radio play was locked into one or other community, and although the band's promotional tactics involved FM radio advertising, it was hard to gain national AM attention.

After a couple of months in the studio doing final overdubs for the album, The Experience set off on a three-month tour, which was sometimes complicated by the reputation which Hendrix's shows had gained for outrageousness and pyromania;

there was a fair amount of paying-off to be done with local police and fire departments. They had very few rest days on a schedule which was arranged to maximize profits, including those from merchandising, which Jeffery had been careful to keep under his control, and which, due to Jimi's image, was highly profitable. Near the end of the tour they rented a house in Los Angeles, where they partied constantly. Their drug use escalated as the drudgery of touring got worse, especially for the road-veteran Hendrix.

Despite his time spent on the road, he did not have a driving licence, but could never resist taking the wheel of a Corvette, of which he bought several. In one incident he was almost killed, when his poor eyesight resulted in him writing off a car, from which he luckily escaped with only minor bruising. He could easily afford the replacement which he bought a couple of days later. Luckily, he could also afford an out of court settlement after hitting a groupie with a brick in Los Angeles.

*Electric Ladyland* was released in October 1968, with The Hollies' *Greatest Hits* and Mary Hopkin's 'Those Were The Days' at the top of the British album and singles charts. Although the album was critically acclaimed, and is even now considered a highpoint of creativity, Hendrix was dissatisfied with the finished product, and had been totally unprepared for the cover picture of 19 naked women on the British Track Records version. He complained to the press that the seriousness of his art was being compromised by the

Jimi with Eric Clapton

Open air groovers at Woodstock

attempts to mirror the 'Wild Man' public image on the album, but the fans did not seem to mind. In America the album entered the charts at number 31 on its way to number 1, with *Are You Experienced?* still in the top ten. To celebrate the band's second birthday they played three nights at Winterland in San Francisco, which were recorded, to be released in 1987.

Despite their popularity, which ensured a top five placing for the single 'All Along The Watchtower', The Experience was becoming more fragmented. Redding was the most dissatisfied, complaining that most of his work ended up being over-dubbed by Hendrix, and responded by being so stoned at some sessions that he could hardly stand. They were beginning to take other directions, Redding with his band Fat Mattress, Mitchell with Mind Octopus, and Hendrix was jamming with a wide variety of musicians, more often including Buddy Miles. Just after Hendrix's 26th birthday party, which included a birthday cake containing more illegal ingredients than the average recipe, Redding and Mitchell returned to London, shortly before The Experience was named as *Billboard*'s top rock band of 1968.

Hendrix was excited by Jeffery's arrangements to buy the lease on a nightclub in New York, The Generation, which were finalized in December. The plan was to add a studio to it, to allow live gigs to be recorded, thus providing a permanent studio for Hendrix to work on his material. The projected cash needs for the

project demanded more touring, however, so a European itinerary was set up
for January 1969, when the band also
reunited for a riotous appearance on the
*Lulu Show* in London. The tour suffered
from some lacklustre performances, and
the band did not have its previous unity,
though a filmed show at the Albert Hall
with Soft Machine and Traffic produced
some memorable moments showing beyond doubt Hendrix's mastery of his art.

Back in America, the projected nightclub
became a state-of-the-art recording studio, bearing in mind that Hendrix's status
as a counter-culture icon would not make
the granting of a club alcohol licence
likely. Eddie Kramer was chosen as the
best person to fit out what would become
Electric Ladyland Studios.

Hendrix was producing for The Buddy Miles Express as well as working on new songs, and enjoying the after-hours at clubs and parties. Hotel rooms would often suffer as a result; on one occasion, one of his party took to Hendrix's room with an axe, causing a great deal of damage. A record company lawyer recalled delivering some papers to Jimi, and finding five girls waiting outside the hotel suite, another answering the door, and one in the bedroom with the star. On another occasion, invited to a society dinner, Hendrix chose the end of the meal to get up on the table and dance, scattering the remaining cutlery and crockery and causing the hostess to faint.

The Experience re-formed for an American tour beginning in April 1969. Jeffery's organization promised the biggest profit-making to date, and an accountant was hired to take care of the gate receipts, which up to now had been taken to the bank in bags and suitcases. In between dates there were rehearsals for the fourth album, but there was no real progress beyond the demo stage. With Eddie Kramer working full-time on Electric Ladyland Studios there was a telling gap in the structure of sessions, not helped by the lack of unity in the band. At one stage Hendrix declared he was not going on with the tour, and was still in New York at 5 pm with a gig to play that night in Detroit. Tour manager Bob Levine persuaded Jimi to play, and scammed a Lear jet to fly him to Detroit by telling the hire company that it was for Frank Sinatra.

There was worse to come. The next day, Hendrix was detained at customs in Toronto when heroin was found in his baggage. This was despite the careful jettisoning of any suspicious substances following a rumour that the authorities were going to pay him special attention. Jimi's reputation was of course well known; he used to receive packets of drugs in the post from well-meaning junkie fans, but the possible damage to major sales resulting from a heroin bust put Jeffery's head into a spin. Due to the possibility of a riot if he did not turn up for the concert, the police allowed Hendrix to play the gig, which passed off well despite his obvious confusion at the day's

On stage at Woodstock

In rehearsal

events. Bail was arranged and the tour proceeded. It moved towards a sell-out night at Madison Square Gardens, whose profits of $75,000 for the evening give an indication of the sort of money Hendrix could bring in by now.

With a break in the tour The Experience went their separate ways, Hendrix going back into the studio with Buddy Miles, and also bringing in Billy Cox on bass. It seems that he needed the stability that came from sessions with his old friends. Maybe playing with black musicians gave him the hope of acceptance by the black population, which seemed for the most part to consider him strange. He believed that his music was the only way he could usefully make any change for the better, although at various times he was put under pressure by the Black Panthers to make a more overt, probably financial, statement in favour of black consciousness.

After the tour Hendrix returned to New York where he was living with his girlfriend Devon Wilson. Their relationship had begun in 1967, and they seemed to be a match for each other's sexual appetite. Jimi had a collection of home movies he called *The Goodbye Films* on which he documented each girl that he had slept with, waving a farewell to him at his door. Devon had a similar though undocumented collection of rock 'n' roll scalps, and her bisexuality gave rise to the rumour that she was in charge of quality control at the head of the queue for a night with Hendrix. Her enthusiasm for drugs matched his; she would often take herself near the limit, and would eventually go too far.

# Woodstock

On 19 June 1969 Hendrix appeared at a court in Toronto for a hearing which fixed a trial date for 8 December. He then went down to California to headline at the Newport Pop Festival, with an appearance fee of $100,000. The Experience had a bad gig, the audience was unforgiving, and Hendrix seemed unable to control his feedback, not helped by an apparently innocent drink which was spiked with acid. He returned to the festival on its

A publicity stunt

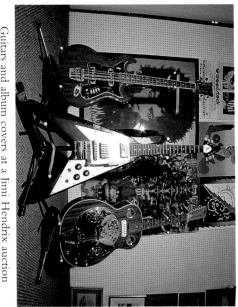

Guitars and album covers at a Jimi Hendrix auction

third day to take part in an unbilled jam
with a group of musicians from different
bands at the event, an act which went a
long way towards offsetting the disaster of
The Experience's set.

Newport was followed by the Denver
Festival, which included sets from Creedence Clearwater Revival, The Mothers
of Invention, Joe Cocker and Iron Butter-
fly. The event was accompanied by a
radical political presence, and crowd trouble came to a head during The Experience's show, with a display of tear-gas and
riot control from the frustrated police
force.

Immediately after the festival Noel Redding, unable to take the bad atmosphere,
as well as being left out of any of the

decision-making, announced his departure from the band. Billy Cox was the obvious replacement, and was introduced as the new bass player during Hendrix's appearance on *The Tonight Show* of 10 July. During his interview, Hendrix described his music in the same terms as religion, and expressed a hope to communicate spirituality through his songs. The live portion of the show was marred by the breakdown of Hendrix's amplifier, but the promotional value of the appearance helped the sales of *Smash Hits*, a compilation including several Hendrix tracks unreleased in America, which was selling well for Warner.

Jeffery could see Hendrix's need for a break, and rented him a house in Shokan, 12 miles from Woodstock. Eddie

Kramer was called in to install some professional recording equipment, and formal jam sessions went on with Billy Cox, percussionists Jerry Velez and Juma Sultan, and guitarist Larry Lee, a multi-cultural mix that Hendrix called Gypsys Suns and Rainbows. There was plenty of drug-taking during the holiday despite the up-coming court case, Hendrix having resigned himself to a probable jail sentence as an example to young people. The band's jamming turned into more serious rehearsals, when Hendrix was announced as the headline act for the festival at Bethel, New York, which would become known as Woodstock. Jimi was the highest paid of an impressive list of artists which included Janis Joplin, The Who, Sly and the Family Stone, Creedence Clearwater Revival and Jefferson Airplane.

Arriving at the festival during the rain of the Sunday, Hendrix fell victim to the drug-infused drinking water, and it was doubtful that he would be able to play. Luckily, the organization of the event had collapsed and he was rescheduled for the following morning, after the official end of the festival. With the daylight exposing the battlefield of the arena, Gypsys Suns and Rainbows, including the returned Mitch Mitchell, took to the stage at the end of the event which has come to symbolize the hippy generation. He was the perfect man for the leading role, the epitome of the free-living experimental age, and performed an unusually long set for the audience. In contrast to the highs of his playing, the band was obviously under-rehearsed, and it was clear that songs written with The Experience were not helped by the increase in band membership. The renditions of 'Star-Spangled Banner' and 'Purple Haze', however remain as a monument to Hendrix's talent at the peak of his career, with 'Star-Spangled Banner' the perfectly timed statement for the anti-war consensus of the counterculture.

Mike Jeffery was, however, a worried man. With the new band obviously unready to take over the mantle of The Experience, the costs of the new studio were escalating and it seemed that his perfect profit-machine might have lost its fuel supply. He booked a short tour of the southern United States, but in a letter of 9 September Hendrix refused to follow his plans. He did agree to a benefit gig for Harlem's United Block Association, arranged through his long-time friends, the Allen twins. It was an attempt to get his music across to the black community, and although his lack of exposure on black radio stations meant that most people there didn't know who he was, he went down well on the day.

After a ramshackle appearance at the Salvation Club for what would be the last gig for Gypsys Suns and Rainbows, Hendrix made the mistake of leaving with Bobby Woods, the club's owner and Jimi's cocaine contact. Woods was murdered the next night by a drugs gang, and Hendrix was kidnapped in order to find out what he knew. Word was sent that he was being well treated, and that he would be released in a couple of days, but Jeffery's hackles were raised, and he called in an underworld favour to bring about Hendrix's immediate return. Jeffery was trying to show that he had control of any situation concerning his artist, but Hendrix shrugged the whole thing off, considering it rather silly. With the increasing number of drugs he was taking, reality was definitely moving into the background.

Mitch Mitchell returned to London in the middle of September, and with Billy Cox the only remaining Gypsy, there was plenty of room for Buddy Miles to step into the breach. Hendrix and Jeffery were scarcely even talking to each other, and Hendrix started to rely on Alan Douglas, a jazz and spoken word producer who had overseen recordings by John Coltrane, Billie Holliday, Lenny Bruce and Alan

Ginsberg. He was married to Hendrix's clothes-designer friend, Stella Douglas, and Hendrix asked him to take control of the jumble that his Record Plant sessions had become. A couple of unscheduled sessions, one with Stephen Stills, another with the Last Poets, were recorded, the latter showing a potential for putting spoken word with music in a way which would not be fully realized until rap found its way into the musical vocabulary. Douglas made an attempt to pair Hendrix with Miles Davis, who was apparently keen to work with Jimi, but at the last minute Davis demanded a $50,000 appearance fee, and the session had to be cancelled.

Douglas seemed to be able to open up Hendrix's creativity for the first time since Chas Chandler had left, but the obvious rapport he was building with Jimi angered the jealous Jeffery. The studio sessions produced new material such as 'Izabella' and 'Room Full of Mirrors' which would be released by Hendrix, Cox and Miles as the Band of Gypsys, though as usual, Hendrix would want to overdub many more times before he was at all happy with the songs. At one point, Warner queried a studio bill for $36,000 for 'Room Full of Mirrors', thinking that it was a total for a completed album. They had to be told gently that it was for a single song.

Hendrix left for the Toronto trial on 8 December, and, in a bizarre repetition, was again arrested for drug possession on the way in to Canada. A capsule was taken away for analysis, and Hendrix's counsel was dumbfounded by the news. Luckily for Jimi, the capsule's contents were of such a strange mix that it could not be classified as a controlled substance, and he was let out of jail. The trial proceeded, with Chas Chandler coming over specially to make a plea on Hendrix's behalf. Hendrix overturned all expectations in his defence by admitting to a list of the various substances that he had taken and the problems that he had, but declaring his innocence in the case of the heroin in his baggage. His up-front approach won him an acquittal.

# Hello and Goodbye

A delighted Hendrix returned to New York, but he was experiencing a creative block in the studio. He was not able to direct himself in this new phase, although he now had the time and resources that he had dreamed of in the days of *Are You Experienced?* However, four New Year concerts at the Fillmore East brought an ecstatic reception for the Band of Gypsys and their latest material, as well as songs from The Experience bag, and the shows were recorded in order to bring out a release on Capitol to fulfil the PPX settlement. The fusion which had entered into the sessions over the last six months came to the fore, as Hendrix's playing crossed over from rock into funk and jazz, showing the creative progress which he had made, as well as indicating the breadth of the ideas that he was trying to bring to life in the studio.

Jeffery's pressure had helped to get Douglas to give up his work with Hendrix, and he began to put the screws on Hendrix to get rid of Buddy Miles, who had the sort of close relationship with Jimi that scared him. The Band of Gypsys was due to play an anti-war benefit at Madison Square Gardens, which turned out to be a disaster. Hendrix was completely stoned, and managed only two songs before sitting on stage and refusing to continue. Jeffery seized his chance, firing Buddy Miles on the spot, an action rooted in reasons both personal – his dislike of the man – and business – he could only see large profits coming in by getting The Experience back together. Having just made the drummer's job available, Jeffery called Noel Redding and offered him Billy Cox's bassist position. An interview with Hendrix, Redding and Mitchell in *Rolling Stone* angled the piece towards the probability of a reunion, although Cox managed to keep his job.

Meanwhile, with the help of a loan from Warners, one studio had been completed at Electric Ladyland. The complex had been designed with Hendrix in mind, and featured white carpeted walls and coloured lights which could be changed according to his mood. He was very proud of the studio, and found it hard to believe that he actually had a share in it. He dived into work on the piles of demos with a new enthusiasm, allowing restrictions to be put on hangers-on, and completing songs with a sense of the old team spirit. Eddie Kramer even managed to keep a ruling on the use of drugs during work, despite the presence of Devon Wilson. As the studio opened for other artists, Hendrix kept Studio A for his constant use, and other engineers knew better than to try to butt in on a Hendrix/Kramer session; most of them were shocked at the 16-hour, unstructured marathons.

Jeffery persuaded Hendrix to play a series of dates around America following the April 1970 release of the *Band of Gypsys* album, which was riding high in the American charts along with Simon and Garfunkel's *Bridge over Troubled Water*. The band was starting to find its live feet, and capacity crowds were appreciative of the rhythmic interplay that Cox brought to the trio, in new numbers like 'Hey Baby' and 'Freedom', which would appear on the *Cry of Love* album, as well as the old favourites. In between gigs, recording continued, and there were enough songs completed for Hendrix to be considering another double album.

Several of the gigs were filmed for Jeffery's planned film, *Rainbow Bridge*, which, due to the soundtrack exclusion in Hendrix's contract with Warner, could be sold to them despite their exclusive rights to the artist. The band flew to Hawaii in July to do some filming, and during one meal with some Warner executives Mitchell spiked the dessert. There followed an impromptu dance session and a viewing of The Beatles' *A Hard Day's Night*, a black and white film which everyone swore was in colour and apparently contained many scenes with a red chicken.

Hendrix was back in the studio in August, trying to finish more tracks before a European tour which he was very unhappy about starting. He was only persuaded to come to the opening party for Electric Ladyland Studios by being promised his lifelong dream of a police escort to the airport to leave for London.

His leave-taking was the last time his friends in America would see him.

Back in a Britain dominated by the rockier sounds of The Beatles' *Let It Be*, Led Zeppelin's *Led Zeppelin II* and The Rolling Stones' *Get Your Ya Yas Out*, Hendrix was booked to play several festivals around Europe, including the Isle of Wight show, which is more famous for being his last concert in England than for any particular musical highlight. Billy Cox started to display signs of paranoia which made his playing completely unpredictable, and he was not helped by a series of unruly concerts, especially a rain-delayed, fight-strewn show at Fehmarn, Germany, which would be the final performance. Cox was put on a plane back to America, and possible replacements were discussed.

On his return to London, Hendrix declared his dissatisfaction with Jeffery, and made enquiries about the possibilities of breaking with his manager, even though such an action might be prohibitively expensive. He visited Chas Chandler, the man with whom Jimi had always felt most at ease, and asked him to come back to work with him. He also rang Eddie Kramer in New York and declared his intention to bring tapes back to London to work on.

During the day of 17 September, he ran several errands, spending most of the time with Monika Dannemann, a West German girlfriend. In the early hours of 18 September he took some sleeping pills, and at 11 am Dannemann noticed that he had been sick, and although his breath-

ing was normal, she could not wake him.
She called an ambulance. By the time he
got to the hospital, the mixture of alcohol
and sleeping tablets had killed him. He was
only 27.

The newspapers leapt upon the death of
the 'wild man of rock', inventing his last
minutes, and Eric Burden declared that
Hendrix had committed suicide, a statement that he later retracted. The stories
surrounding his death built a wall
around his work which would hide it
for several years. Amidst all the publicity, Hendrix was buried in Seattle on 1
October 1970. He left behind him a
mountain of half-finished work, a musical legacy which has made him one of
the giants of the modern age, and which
adds poignancy to his last lyrics: 'This

story of/life is quicker/than the wink of
an eye/The story of love/is hello and
goodbye/Until we meet again.'